You Know You're Getting Old When . . .

Emma Burgess

summersdale

Copyright © Summersdale Publishers Ltd, 2003
Reprinted 2003

Text by Emma Burgess. Cartoons by Kate Taylor.

Summersdale Publishers Ltd
46 West Street
Chichester
West Sussex
PO19 1RP
UK

www.summersdale.com

ISBN 1 84024 374 0

Printed and bound in the UK.

You know you're getting old when . . .

Every sentence starts with
'In my day … '

You remember the Coronation.
Wasn't George VI dashing?

You think the Internet
is something fishermen use.

You think a 'mobile' is a phone
on wheels.

Your 'rosebuds' – as your
husband used to call them –
are now more like
hanging baskets.

You drink too much ... tea.

Even golf wears you out.

You would record *Songs of Praise*
… if only you could
work the video.

You grumble about how nice
the old-style British passports
were – even though you've never
left the country.

You still refer to the EU as
the EEC, and can't see how
it fits into the British Empire.

You try and talk into your
TV's remote control.

You would definitely fail your
driving test if you had to take it
these days. Cars have engines
now for a start.

The mention of KY Jelly
no longer makes you laugh.

You keep abreast of the
latest fashions by popping
into your local branch of
Past Times every now and then.

Your choice of shoe wear is
determined by what your
doctor prescribes for you …

… come to think of it, so is
your choice of underwear.

Your slippers are more worn
down than your shoes.

You have more plastic in your
hips than in your wallet.

You are not worried about
losing the Pound to the Euro …

… you're still busy trying to cope
with decimalisation.

You consider buying a
sports car for weekends –
a Reliant Robin would be
perfect.

You get asked your age
on the bus.

You think Alan
Titchmarsh is sexy.

You are still collecting
Green Shield *Stamps*.
Bless.

Going bald is no longer
a worry for you … your
husband's losing his
eyesight at last.

You think that modern air travel
isn't safe enough. I mean, just
look at the *Hindenberg*.

Your application for *Blind Date*
is turned down – they don't
do the one for oldies any more.

You're so hot in bed.
Aren't electric blankets great?

The specs you wear are thicker
than glass bricks.

You have so many age spots,
your grandchildren regularly
play 'join the dots' … to find
they make an old person.

You panic when friends threaten
to organise a birthday party
for you … because your lungs
failed the last time you tried
to blow out all those candles.

You still enjoy sport, but you've swapped your weights for a pair of knitting needles.

You wear a hat, scarf
and full-length coat to
keep out that August chill.

Your idea of being irresponsible
is spending your weekly pension
on something other than
food and heating.

You recall your happy teenage
memories in black and white.

Your baby pictures
are in sepia.

You think that buying stuff
'online' is exclusive to
trapeze artists.

You can recite the ingredients
of every anti-wrinkle cream
on the market.

You are saving up for
Cryogenic Preservation.

Policemen seem younger
than your kids.

The smutty jokes you
used to tell now appear
on Kiddies TV.

You're a regular on shows like *Trisha* and *Kilroy* – along with the rest of the bus load from the Old People's Home.

When people hear you muttering under your breath about 'kids today' they don't realise you're talking about 40-year-olds.

Your home videos are
shot in cine-film.

Beige contains all the
spectrums of your rainbow.

You remember the days
when Coca-Cola still
contained cocaine.

And Opium was something you inhaled, not splashed behind your ears.

You think your new,
totally nondescript jacket
is really snazzy.

You are ready to retire … from
retirement itself.

You audition as the Thora Hird
replacement in the chair lift ads,
but are rejected because
you're too old.

You're no longer into politics.
Not since your favourite MP -
Mr Gladstone - retired.

You have terrible dry rot …
you really ought to
see the doctor.

Anyone with hair
seems young.

You stop on the
motorway hard shoulder …
to admire the view.

You think that the problem of
transport pollution could
be eased by shovelling up all
the horse dung.

Your idea of Modern Art
is cave drawings.

You think satellite TV is something that only the crew of *Apollo 13* could receive.

Your hair comes out
of a can.

You refuse to believe that
woman have the vote.

You start to reminisce about major incidents in your youth. The Boer War affects you to this day.

You've not yet mastered
modern plumbing. Those tin
baths in front of the
fire are a bind.

You can't see the point of
flushing toilets. It's just as easy
to tip your bed-pan out
of the window.

You cancel your subscription to
What Car?
and replace it with one for
What Wheelchair?

You have a sticker in the
back of your car that reads
'My other one's a horse and cart'.

You start keeping budgerigars …
… and actually enjoying their
company.

Your idea of a great Friday
night is a jug of mead at
the local tavern.

A car alarm in the street
goes off and you rush to the
nearest air-raid shelter.

You no longer apologise for
farting … actually, you
don't even notice.

You have trouble parking your
Rover Metro.

Your kids are going
bald and grey.

Funeral directors try
to befriend you.

Your friends admire you because
you still have a full set of teeth …
… they're not to know you
keep them in a drawer.

You've forgotten the
Language of Love, but you're
fluent in Bingo Lingo.

Your idea of extravagant is
having your will translated into
several different languages.

You give up smoking to save money … Woodbines aren't cheap, you know.

Your children are planning their
retirement parties.

You're not aware that your
car has more than one gear.
First seems to get you everywhere
you want to go.

You don't need to visit your
dentist anymore … you just send
him your teeth in the post.

www.summersdale.com